Table of Contents

Introduction

Direct Teaching of Spelling

Regardless of the reading philosophy or program used in a school, all children benefit by direct teaching of spelling. This instruction may be a block of time set aside strictly for spelling instruction or an integrated part of a whole language program.

In recent years, the concept of invented spelling has been a controversial topic. Invented spelling does provide students with a tool to begin expressing themselves in written form. However, at some point direct teaching of spelling needs to begin.

Students need to be taught the following:
- how to spell words that are created using English phonemes, as well as common nonphonetic words
- learning strategies to help them spell difficult words
- that correct spelling increases their ability to communicate their ideas and feelings to others

Using This Book

The 30 spelling units contain these components:
- a reproducible list of 10 spelling words
- two sentences for dictation
- four reproducible activity pages for practicing the spelling list words

A reproducible testing sheet is included on page 146. It contains lines for the 10 spelling words, for two special words you may have assigned, for two dictation sentences, and three lines that can be used to give review words of your choice from preceding lists.

These components may be placed in a special spelling folder with the student's record sheet (see page 145) attached to use as a working portfolio.

Detailed information on each component is given on pages 5 and 6.

The spelling lists can be used for whole-class, small-group, or individual instruction. However the lessons are used, start where the students are. Spelling lists 1-12 contain predominantly short and long vowel words. Later lessons introduce vowel digraphs, blends, and more complex special words.

Most first graders are not ready for formal spelling lessons before the middle of the school year. When you do begin using directed spelling lessons, choose those lists or words that meet their needs. Some second grade students will need to begin with spelling list 1. Others will be ready to begin with later lessons.

Following Student Progress
The Table of Contents contains the skills covered in these spelling lessons. Class and individual record forms (pages 144 and 145) are provided to help you track student progress.

Create Your Own Activities for Spelling Lists
Use the blank forms (pages 147-149) to create spelling lists, configuration puzzles, and word sorts with words from units of study, special holiday words, or words containing a specific phonetic element or skill needing further practice. These forms may also be used to create student-selected spelling lists.

Spelling Unit Components

Word List *(pages 11-20)*

Reproduce the spelling list twice for each student—one copy to use at school and one copy to take home along with the parent letter (page 150).

Students use the list at school for "partner practice" (see page 7), independent practice, and to copy into individual spelling dictionaries (see page 8).

Name:
on
not
but
at
had
in
did
get
red
hot

Sentences for Dictation *(pages 21-23)*

There are two dictation sentences for each spelling list. Space for sentence dictation is provided on the test form (see page 146). Ask students to listen to the complete sentence as you read it. They then repeat it out loud. Give the sentence in phrases, repeating each phrase one time clearly. Have students repeat the phrase. Wait as students write the phrase.

Activity Pages

Four reproducible pages are provided for each spelling list. These can be used as teacher-directed lessons, for partner practice, or as individual assignments.

 Read, Write, & Spell

This page is used for the initial practice of each spelling word. The student spells one word at a time following these steps:

Step 1 - Trace the word and spell it aloud. (Some children will need guidance in learning how to do this softly.)

Step 2 - Copy the word onto the first blank line and spell it again.

Step 3 - Fold the paper along the fold line to cover the spelling words. (Only the last blank line should be seen.) Write the word from memory.

Step 4 - Open the paper and check the spelling. (This is a <u>very</u> important step. Children need to learn to self-correct so misspellings are not being practiced.) Repeat the steps for each spelling word.

Building Spelling Skills			
Name:		Spelling List	
	Trace	**Write**	**Spell and Check**
1.	on	_____	_____
2.	not	_____	_____
3.	but	_____	_____
4.	at	_____	_____
5.	had	_____	_____
6.	in	_____	_____
7.	did	_____	_____
8.	get	_____	_____
9.	red	_____	_____
10.	hot	_____	_____
11.		_____	_____
12.		_____	_____

You may want to put the directions for activity 1 on a chart to post in the classroom.

1. Trace and Spell
2. Copy and Spell
3. Cover and Spell
4. Uncover and Check

         Building Spelling Skills 1-2 EMC 725

Visual Memory

Configuration puzzles help the student become aware of the shape and order of the letters in a word. This improves visual memory.

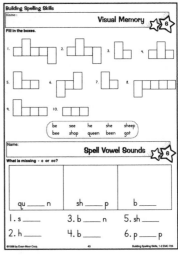

Other Skills

A variety of other skills are practiced on the bottom half of the page. These include editing for correct spelling, rhyming words, adding endings, and practicing phonetic elements.

Word Meaning

Students complete this page to show an understanding of the meaning of the words. Some pages require the filling in of blanks; others ask students to answer questions.

Word Study

The phonetic and word analysis skills on this page may be used as a direct teaching lesson or as independent practice. Many of the pages involve sorting words by phonetic elements. Students cut out the word cards, read them, and then paste the cards in the correct column.

More Ideas for Spelling Practice

Practice with Teacher

Give a pretest to see what types of errors are being made by students. Explain that this is a way to learn what needs to be practiced. It is not a "test" that will be graded in any way. Write each word on a chart or an overhead transparency and have students correct their own papers so they can see where they need practice. Use these errors as a guide for the development of minilessons on specific skills or phonemes.

Practice with a Partner

Have students work in pairs to practice their spelling lists. One student gives the word aloud, pronouncing it carefully. The other student writes the word. The "tester" then spells the word aloud as the writer checks to see if the word was spelled correctly. Any word missed is written correctly before continuing. After the list is completed, students change roles and repeat the activity.

Extending Use of Spelling Words

1. Have students use the words on their spelling lists in their own writings, both in isolated sentences and in stories and reports.

2. Have students find their spelling words in other places such as posters and charts in the classroom, in literature books, and in magazines or newspapers.

3. Encourage students to find other words that contain the same sound or pattern being studied in the spelling lesson.

Create a Word-Rich Room Environment

You can improve students' spelling by filling your classroom with words. Provide opportunities for hearing language (talk, tell stories, read to them) and for seeing words (post banners, charts, lists of words, student writings; provide literature books, nonfiction books, magazines, etc.).

Write! Write! Write!

A student's writings serve two purposes. They give students a chance to use the language and spelling skills being learning. They provide the teacher with clues to the student's understanding of sound/letter relationships and can help identify which phonetic elements and special spellings need to be practiced.

You will begin to see fewer invented spellings as students transfer new phonetic or structural understandings from the spelling lessons into their writing experiences.

Student Spelling Dictionaries

Self-made spelling dictionaries provide students with a reference for the spelling of words they frequently use in their writing.

Materials to Use:
- copy of "My Own Spelling Dictionary" form (page 9)
- 26 sheets lined paper—6" x 9" (15 x 23 cm)
- 2 sheets construction paper or tagboard for cover —6" x 9" (15 x 23 cm)
- stapler
- masking tape

Steps to Follow:
1. Color and cut out the cover sheet form. Glue it to the front cover of the dictionary.

2. Staple the lined paper inside the cover. Place masking tape over the staples.

3. Guide students (or ask parent volunteers) to write a letter of the alphabet on each page.

What to Include:
1. When students ask for the correct spelling of a special word, have them write it in their dictionary.

2. Include special words being learned as part of science or social studies units.

3. Include words for special holidays.

4. Include the common words students continue to misspell on tests and in daily written work.

5. Add color and number words if these are not on charts posted in the classroom.

Aa Bb Cc Dc Ee Ff Gg Hh Ii Jj

Kk Ll Mm Nn Oo Pp

My Own Spelling Dictionary

_____

Aa Bb Cc Dd Ee Ff G

Qq Rr Ss Tt Uu Vv Ww Xx Yy Zz

Aa Bb Cc Dc Ee Ff Gg Hh Ii Jj

Kk Ll Mm Nn Oo Pp

My Own Spelling Dictionary

_____

Aa Bb Cc Dd Ee Ff G

Qq Rr Ss Tt Uu Vv Ww Xx Yy Zz

Spelling Strategies

Learning a few simple strategies can help students become better spellers. Teach the strategies one at a time using appropriate words from the spelling lists. List each strategy on a chart as it is introduced. Post the chart as a helpful reminder to students. Review the strategies frequently to help students internalize them.

Say a word correctly.	Don't leave out or mispronounce sounds. Write the sounds in the correct order.
Think about what the word looks like.	Think about how the spelling pattern looks. Write it, look at it, decide if it looks correct.
Look for small words in spelling words.	spin - pin, in cupcake - cup, cake
Use rhyming words to help spell a word.	If you can spell book, you can spell look.
Use rules for adding endings.	Drop silent *e* before adding suffix. Double the final consonant before adding suffix.
Think about what the word means.	Some words sound the same, but have different meanings and are spelled in different ways. Match the spelling with its meaning.
Use outside help.	Use charts, banners, and lists around the classroom. Ask someone for help. Use a personal spelling dictionary.

Name:

on

not

but

at

had

in

did

get

red

hot

Name:

as

has

fox

box

mix

egg

jam

pet

nap

big

cut

Name:

his

is

an

and

can

all

call

land

hand

small

cut

Name: 	Name: 	Name:
up	add	be
it	ask	see
him	came	he
I	save	she
for	name	sheep
or	ride	shop
four	bone	queen
we	kite	been
man	cute	got
men	mine	bee

 **7**

  **8**

  **9**

no	a	some
go	that	come
going	the	home
so	them	fun
do	day	funny
doing	may	ran
most	made	run
kind	was	use
find	of	us
gave	if	running

cut

place

make

making

help

here

want

nice

to

two

into

send

back

end

both

fast

last

must

just

bath

black

cut

went

sent

take

like

time

didn't

puppy

candy

by

my

cut

less

tell

will

still

letter

little

off

well

silly

happy

boat

float

coat

long

along

belong

paw

fawn

tall

wall

way

away

today

play

played

chain

chase

paint

wait

rain

cut

cut

too	now	her
good	down	girl
book	how	turn
shook	out	hurt
school	shout	first
soon	about	were
what	our	card
when	house	part
who	slow	start
took	show	are

cut

cut

more	have	you
store	give	yes
stand	love	yell
star	from	drop
blew	live	line
new	friend	side
flew	much	your
stone	such	dress
sting	old	draw
ring	told	saw

cut

cut

boy	this	why
toy	then	try
oil	these	trying
soil	thing	fly
boil	think	eat
mother	thank	mean
father	with	each
sister	bank	read
brother	sing	treat
other	wish	sunny

trip	stick	birthday
tree	trick	people
train	quick	present
hop	back	candle
stop	zoo	cake
stopped	root	children
said	look	gifts
say	looked	party
number	pack	game
one	cook	bring

cut

cut

Building Spelling Skills 1-2 EMC 725

put	they	over
push	their	under
pull	than	before
could	many	after
would	any	again
found	anything	inside
round	very	outside
around	because	which
something	know	where
brown	water	there

cut

cut

Sentences for Dictation

List 1

    1. Tom **did not get** a **hot** bun.
    2. Kim **had on** a **red** hat.

List 2

    1. His **pet fox** was in a **big box**.
    2. Ann **has jam** and an **egg**.

List 3

    1. **Is his hand small**?
    2. Bob **can call his** mom **and** dad.

List 4

    1. **I** got **it for him**.
    2. Can **four men** go **up** in a jet?

List 5

    1. Lee **came** to **ask** for a **ride**.
    2. **Save** a **bone** for the **cute** dog.

List 6

    1. I **got** to **see** the **queen bee**.
    2. Can **he** get **sheep** in the pet **shop**?

List 7

    1. A **kind** man **gave** us his dog.
    2. Am I **going** to **find** the **most** eggs?

List 8

    1. Max **made that** kite for **them**.
    2. **Was the day** hot?

List 9

    1. **Come** and see the **funny** cat **running home**.
    2. **Some** hens **ran** up to **us**.

List 10

    1. **Help** me get the **two** pigs **into** the pen.
    2. I **want** to **make** a **nice place here** to sit.

List 11

1. Tim and Sam **both** ran **fast** at the **end**.
2. She **must send** the **black** hat **back**.

List 12

1. I **liked** the note he **sent** me.
2. The bus **went by my** stop on **time**.

List 13

1. **Tell** the **happy little** puppy to sit **still**.
2. **Will** the name come **off** that **letter**?

List 14

1. The **fawn** ran **along** the **tall wall**.
2. Did that **boat belong** to the man in a **long coat**?

List 15

1. We had to **wait** for the **rain** to go **away**.
2. Is he going to **play** games and **paint today**?

List 16

1. **Who took** that **good book** to **school**?
2. He **shook** the box to see **what** was in it.

List 17

1. Do not **shout** in **our house**.
2. **Slow down** and tell me **about** the **show**.

List 18

1. The **girl hurt part** of **her** leg.
2. Jim and Ann **were** going to **start** the **card** game.

List 19

1. A **new ring** at the **store** has a **stone** like a **star**.
2. **Stand** still or the bee will **sting** you.

List 20

1. Did he **give** the note to his **old friend**?
2. I **live such** a long way **from** here.

List 21

1. Did Mom **yell** when she **saw you draw** on **your dress**?
2. **Drop** the ball on that **side** of the **line**.

List 22

1. **Father** gave the **other boy** a new **toy**.
2. My **brother** and **sister** dug in the **soil**.

List 23

1. **Thank** you for **this bank** and **these** toys.
2. **Sing** a song and **then** make a **wish**.

List 24

1. **Why** is the **mean** frog **trying** to get that **fly**?
2. Will you **read** to me as I **eat** this **treat**?

List 25

1. Lee took a **trip** on **train number one**.
2. Can you **hop** to the **tree** and then **stop**?

List 26

1. We **looked** at Pete do a **trick** with a **stick**.
2. Will the **cook** put the food back in his **pack**?

List 27

1. The **children** will play a **game** and eat **cake** at the **party**.
2. Will **people bring gifts** for my **birthday**?

List 28

1. Mark **found something brown** under the tree.
2. **Could** you help me **pull** my wagon **around** the yard?

List 29

1. **Many** children went home **because** it was **very** late.
2. Did **they** put **anything** in the **water**?

List 30

1. Put the box **inside** that car **over** there.
2. Which dog is running **outside under** the trees?

Name:

Spelling List

Trace	Write	Spell and Check
1. on	_____	_____
2. not	_____	_____
3. but	_____	_____
4. at	_____	_____
5. had	_____	_____
6. in	_____	_____
7. did	_____	_____
8. get	_____	_____
9. red	_____	_____
10. hot	_____	_____
11. _____	_____	_____

fold

special word

_____

special word

         Building Spelling Skills 1-2 EMC 725

Building Spelling Skills

Fill in the boxes.

1.

2.

on	not	but	at	had
in	did	get	red	hot

3.

4.

5.

6.

7.

8.

9.

10.

Name: _____

Find the Mistake

1

Put an X on the misspelled words.

1. The pan is hat.

2. A dog is un the bed.

3. Can I git a cat?

4. His hat is read.

Name:

Word Meaning

Write the missing word on the line.

1. Is the hat _____ and green?

    hot   red   had

2. Set the box_____ top of the desk.

    in   at   on

3. Can you _____ a cup for me?

    get   but   hot

4. _____ Ann get on the bus?

    Not   Did   Had

5. His pizza is _____.

    but   hot   not

6. Dad _____ to fix the car.

    in   at   had

Write sentences with these words.

Building Spelling Skills

Name:

Cut out the word cards.
Read the words.
Glue the words in the correct boxes.

a	e	i	o	u

on	in	not	did	but
get	at	hot	red	had
cup	sit	men	pan	up

27   Building Spelling Skills 1-2 EMC 725

Name:

Spelling List

Trace	**Write**	**Spell and Check**
1. as		
2. has		
3. fox		
4. box		
5. mix		
6. egg		
7. jam		
8. pet		
9. nap		
10. big		
11. _____		
special word		

_____
special word

fold

Name:

Visual Memory

Fill in the boxes.

1.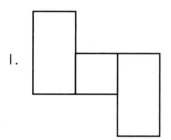

2.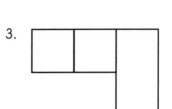

3.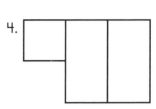

4.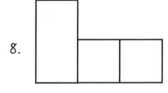

5.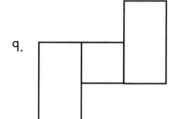

6.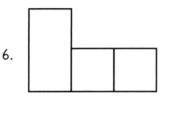

7.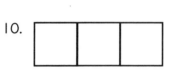

8.

9.

10.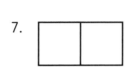

| as | has | fox | box | mix |
| egg | jam | pet | nap | big |

Name:

Spell Vowel Sounds

Fill in the missing vowel.

a e i o u

f __ x   j __ m   b __ x

__ gg   __ s   h __ s

m __ x   n __ p   p __ t

b __ g

| as | has | fox | box | mix |
| egg | jam | pet | nap | big |

Building Spelling Skills 1-2 EMC 725

Name:

Word Meaning

2

Fill in the missing word.

as   has   fox   box   mix   egg   jam   pet   nap   big

1. A _____ was in the _____.

2. The hen has a _____ _____ in the nest.

3. Mom ate _____ on a bun.

4. Ned _____ to take a _____.

5. Can you _____ up the paint?

6. Ann has a _____ cat.

Write sentences with these words.

Name:

Word Study

2

Mark the words with the same vowel sound.

1. jam   box   nap   has

2. pet   egg   mix   red

3. box   as   fox   got

4. it   mix   pet   rip

Write the spelling words that rhyme.

1. fox _____

2. has _____

3. get _____

4. pig _____

5. fix _____

as	big	box	egg	fox
has	jam	mix	nap	pet

          Building Spelling Skills 1-2 EMC 725

Building Spelling Skills

Name:

Spelling List

Trace	Write	Spell and Check
1. is		
2. his		
3. an		
4. and		
5. can		
6. all		
7. call		
8. land		
9. small		
10. hand		
11. _____ special word		

fold

_____ special word

Building Spelling Skills

Name: _____

Visual Memory

Fill in the boxes.

1. ▢▢▢▢▢

2. ▢▢▢▢

3. ▢▢▢

4. ▢▢▢

5. ▢▢▢

6. ▢▢▢

7. ▢▢

8. ▢▢▢▢

9. ▢▢▢▢

10. ▢▢

| his | is | an | and | can |
| all | call | land | hand | small |

Name: _____

Spell Correctly

Unscramble the letters.

na _____   allsm _____   nac _____

si _____   nad _____   nahd _____

llac _____   shi _____   lal _____

andl _____

| all | an | hand | call | can |
| and | his | is | land | small |

Name:

Word Meaning

3

Fill in the missing word.

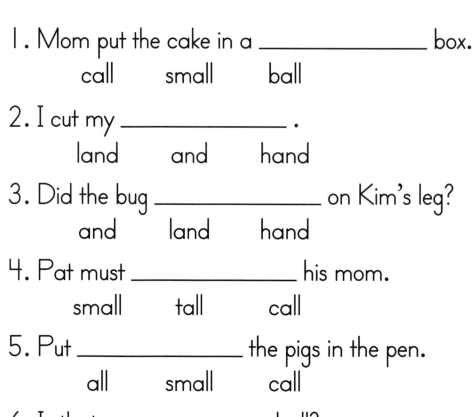

1. Mom put the cake in a _____ box.

    call   small   ball

2. I cut my _____ .

    land   and   hand

3. Did the bug _____ on Kim's leg?

    and   land   hand

4. Pat must _____ his mom.

    small   tall   call

5. Put _____ the pigs in the pen.

    all   small   call

6. Is that _____ ball?

    is   and   his

Write sentences with these words.

Building Spelling Skills 1-2 EMC 725

Building Spelling Skills

Name:

Word Study

3

Cut out the cards.
Read the words.
Paste them in the boxes.

the sound of *a* in *an*	the sound of *a* in *all*

can	cat	small	and
fawn	call	want	has
land	saw	hand	ball

Name:

Trace	**Write**	**Spell and Check**
1. up		
2. it		
3. him		
4. I		
5. or		
6. for		
7. four		
8. we		
9. man		
10. men		
11. _____		

special word

_____

special word

fold

Name:

Visual Memory

4

Fill in the boxes.

1.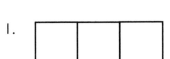

2.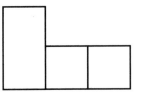

3.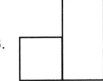

4.

5.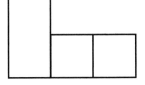

6.

7.

8.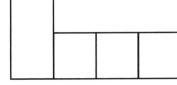

9.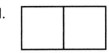

10.

up	it	him	I	for
or	four	we	man	men

Name:

Find the Mistake

4

Circle the words that are misspelled.

1. Tim has ⭕for dogs.

2. That min had a hat.

3. Can wee go with them?

4. Is the cake four me?

5. Did Nina see hem?

Name:

Word Meaning

4

Fill in the missing word.

| up | it | him | I | for | or | four | we | man | men |

1. I want _____ cookies.

2. The red cap is _____ Tammy.

3. A _____ got on the bus.

4. Four _____ got off the bus.

5. Jose and _____ went to the zoo.

6. An ape went _____ in the tree.

Write sentences with these words.

[ ] _____

_____

[ ] _____

_____

Building Spelling Skills

Name: _____

Change a letter to make a new word.

_____ an	_____ an	_____ an
_____ en	_____ en	_____ en
_____ oat	_____ oat	_____ oat

Building Spelling Skills 1-2 EMC 725

Name:

Spelling List

5

Trace	Write	Spell and Check
1. add	_____	_____
2. ask	_____	_____
3. came	_____	_____
4. name	_____	_____
5. ride	_____	_____
6. bone	_____	_____
7. save	_____	_____
8. kite	_____	_____
9. cute	_____	_____
10. mine	_____	_____
11. _____	_____	_____

fold

special word

_____
special word

Name:

Visual Memory

Fill in the boxes.

1.
2.
3.
4.

5.
6.
7.
8.

9.
10.

add   ask   came   save   name   ride   bone   kite   cute   mine

Name:

Find the Correct Word

Circle the word that is spelled correctly.

1. kame   (came)
2. ask   aks
3. kite   kyte
4. ridd   ride
5. qute   cute

6. bone   bown
7. myne   mine
8. add   adde
9. zave   save
10. naim   name

Building Spelling Skills

Name: _____

Word Meaning

Fill in the missing word.

1. The _____ kitten jumped on the bed.

     mine   cute   add   came

2. _____ that _____ for the dog.

     Ask   Save   bone   name

3. That red _____ is _____.

     mine   add   save   kite

4. Did you _____ to _____ his bike?

     add   ask   came   ride

5. His _____ is Max.

     came   name   save   mine

Write sentences with these words.

	_____
_____	
	_____
_____	

Building Spelling Skills

Name: _____

Cut out the cards.
Read the words.
Paste them in the boxes.

Write the words in the correct boxes

long vowel sounds	short vowel sounds

add	came	ride	up
him	save	cute	men
ask	bone	can	name
got	hand	mine	kite

Name:

Spelling List

6

Trace	Write	Spell and Check
1. be	_____	_____
2. see	_____	_____
3. got	_____	_____
4. she	_____	_____
5. sheep	_____	_____
6. shop	_____	_____
7. queen	_____	_____
8. been	_____	_____
9. bee	_____	_____
10. he	_____	_____
11. _____	_____	_____

fold

special word

_____

special word

Building Spelling Skills

Name: _____

Visual Memory

Fill in the boxes.

1.

2.

3.

4.

5.

6.

7.

8.

9.

10.

| be | see | he | she | sheep |
| bee | shop | queen | been | got |

Name: _____

Spell Vowel Sounds

What is missing—e or ee?

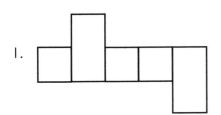

qu ___ ___ n   sh ___ ___ p   b ___ ___ ___

1. s ___   3. b ___ n   5. sh ___

2. h ___   4. b ___   6. p ___ p

Name:

Word Meaning

6

Fill in the missing word.

---

she   sheep   shop   queen

---

1. The _____ has three white _____.

2. _____ keeps the sheep in a pen.

3. The queen got them at a _____.

---

see   he   been   bee

---

1. Has Jim _____ in the garden?

2. A big _____ sat on a red bud.

3. Did _____ _____ the bee?

Write sentences with these words.

Building Spelling Skills

Word Study

6

Cut out the cards.
Read the words.
Paste them in the boxes.

the sound of *e* in *me*	the sound of *e* in *pet*

be	get	see	queen
hen	mess	she	sheep
bell	bee	red	then

47   Building Spelling Skills 1-2 EMC 725

Name:

Spelling List

7

Trace	Write	Spell and Check
1. no	_____	_____
2. go	_____	_____
3. going	_____	_____
4. most	_____	_____
5. kind	_____	_____
6. find	_____	_____
7. gave	_____	_____
8. so	_____	_____
9. do	_____	_____
10. doing	_____	_____
11. _____		

fold

special word

_____

special word

Building Spelling Skills

Fill in the boxes.

1.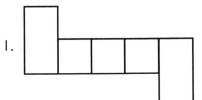

2.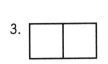

3.

4.

5.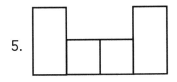

6.

7.

8.

9.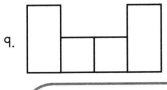

10.

no   go   going   most   so   do   doing   kind   find   gave

---

Name: _____

Make New Words

7

Change a letter.

| no | __s__ o |
| cave | ___ ave |

| mind | ___ ind |
| post | ___ ost |

Add an ending.

go _____going_____   find _____

do _____   sleep _____

Name:

Word Meaning

⭐ ⭐ 7

Fill in the missing word.

1. What is that man _____?

    going   doing   find

2. Miss Green is a _____ woman.

    find   most   kind

3. We are _____ to Disneyland.

    doing   go   going

4. Mom _____ me a new lunch box.

    gave   find   do

5. I did _____ of my homework.

    so   kind   most

6. Can you help me _____ my lost dog?

    kind   going   find

7. Tonya needs _____ go home now.

    so   to   do

Write sentences with these words.

	_____
	_____
	_____
	_____

Name:

Word Study

7

Cut out the words.
Paste them in the correct boxes.

sound of *o* in *no*	sound of *i* in *my*	sound of *a* in *cave*	sound of *o* in *too*

kind	gave	most	cake
do	to	so	find
save	go	mine	blue

Name:

Spelling List

8

Trace	Write	Spell and Check
1. the	_____	_____
2. that	_____	_____
3. them	_____	_____
4. day	_____	_____
5. may	_____	_____
6. made	_____	_____
7. was	_____	_____
8. of	_____	_____
9. if	_____	_____
10. a	_____	_____
11. _____	_____	_____

special word

_____

special word

fold

Building Spelling Skills 1-2 EMC 725

Building Spelling Skills

Visual Memory

Fill in the boxes.

1.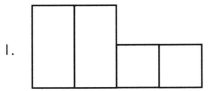

2.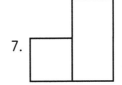

3.

4.

5.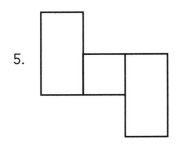

6.

7.

8.

9.

10.

day	of	them	if
that	was	made	the
may	a		

Name:

Find the Correct Word

Circle the word that is spelled correctly.

1. taht   that
2. may   mai
3. the   duh
4. mayd   made
5. wus   was
6. dae   day
7. thm   them
8. of   ov

Name:

Word Meaning

Fill in the missing words.

day	of	them	if	a
that	was	made	the	may

1. Sunday is the first _____ of the week.

2. May I have _____ slice of cake?

3. Ask if you _____ come to my house.

4. Grandmother _____ a cake for them.

5. Will _____ boys win the game?

6. What is in _____ big box?

7. Bob will come with us _____ he has time.

8. The little boy's balloon _____ red.

Write sentences with these words.

Name:

Word Study

Cut out the word cards.
Read the words.
Glue the words in the correct boxes.

sound of *a* in *came*	sound of *a* in *hat*

may	stay	flake	sand
play	cake	plant	game
sat	cape	pan	day

Name:

Spelling List

Trace	Write	Spell and Check
1. some		
2. come		
3. home		
4. fun		
5. funny		
6. run		
7. running		
8. ran		
9. us		
10. use		
11. _____		
special word		

fold

_____
special word

Building Spelling Skills

Name: _____

Visual Memory

Fill in the boxes.

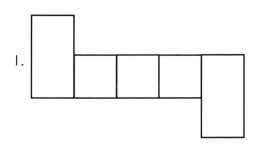

1. [   ][   ][   ][   ][   ]

2. [   ][   ][   ][   ]

3. 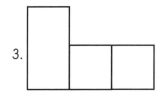 [   ][   ][   ]

4. [   ][   ][   ][   ]   5. [   ][   ][   ]   6. [   ][   ][   ]   7. [   ][   ]

8. [   ][   ][   ][   ][   ][   ]   9. [   ][   ][   ]   10. [   ][   ][   ]

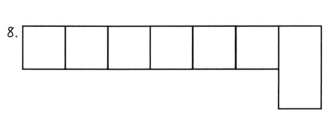

some	come	home	fun	funny
ran	run	use	us	running

Name: _____

Making New Words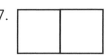

Write the last letter two times.
Then add *ing* to the word.

run + n + ing = <u>running</u>

1. run _____   5. cut _____

2. hit _____   6. tap _____

3. hum _____   7. rub _____

4. tag _____   8. sit _____

Name:

Word Meaning

9

Fill in the missing word.

some	come	home	fun	funny
ran	run	use	us	running

1. Can you go to the circus with _____?

2. I _____ to the circus tent.

3. Sid and Tina were _____ too.

4. Will the clowns _____ here?

5. The _____ clowns jumped up and down.

6. _____ clowns were in a little car.

7. We had _____ at the circus.

8. It is time to go _____ .

Write sentences with these words.

_____

_____

_____

_____

Building Spelling Skills

Name:

Cut out the cards.
Read the words.
Paste them in the boxes.

the sound of *u* in *up*	the sound of *o* in *no*

some	home	stone	fun
come	bone	don't	jump
joke	run	us	boat

Building Spelling Skills 1-2 EMC 725

Name:

10

Trace	Write	Spell and Check
1. place	_____	_____
2. make	_____	_____
3. making	_____	_____
4. help	_____	_____
5. here	_____	_____
6. want	_____	_____
7. nice	_____	_____
8. to	_____	_____
9. two	_____	_____
10. into	_____	_____
11. _____	_____	_____

fold

special word

special word

Building Spelling Skills

Visual Memory

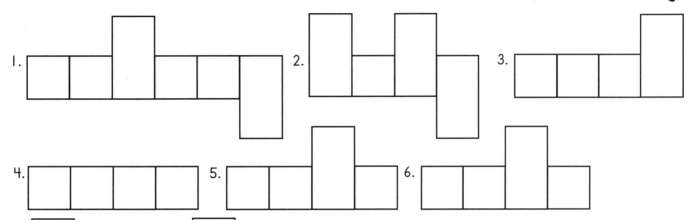

Name:

Fill in the boxes.

1.
2.
3.
4.
5.
6.
7.
8.
9.
10.

place	make	help	here
want	nice	to	two
	into	making	

Find the Mistake

Name:

Put an X on the misspelled words.

1. hep   help

2. make   mak

3. intwo   into

4. nize   nice

5. place   plaic

6. makking   making

7. twe   two

8. here   heer

9. wunt   want

10. to   tou

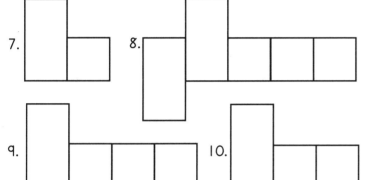

Name:

Word Meaning

10

Fill in the missing word.

1. Can you _____ me _____ a cake?

      here   help   making   make

2. That is a _____ pet hamster.

      makes   two   nice   into

3. I _____ _____ cookies.

      to   two   make   want

4. Let's go _____ the mall.

      two   here   to   place

5. Toss the ball _____ the hoop.

      to   two   here   into

6. _____ is the _____ to get ice cream.

      Help   Here   place   make

Write sentences with these words.

Name:

Word Study

10

Make a new word.

• Add **ing.**

play + ing = playing

• Drop silent **e.** Add **ing.**

make + ing = making

1. bake _____

2. want _____

3. sing _____

4. ride _____

5. take _____

6. start _____

7. wash _____

8. come _____

9. chase _____

10. smile _____

The clown is _____.

smile

Dad is _____.

bake

Anna is _____.

sing

 Building Spelling Skills 1-2 EMC 725

Name: _____

Spelling List

11

Trace	Write	Spell and Check
1. send	_____	_____
2. back	_____	_____
3. end	_____	_____
4. bath	_____	_____
5. fast	_____	_____
6. last	_____	_____
7. both	_____	_____
8. must	_____	_____
9. just	_____	_____
10. black	_____	_____
11. _____	_____	_____

fold

special word

_____

special word

Building Spelling Skills

Visual Memory

11

Fill in the boxes.

1.

2.

3.

4.

5.

6.

7.

8.

9.

10.

send	back	end	both
fast	last	must	just
	bath	black	

Rhyming Words

11

Write the words that rhyme.

back   end   fast   must

_____   _____   _____   _____

_____   _____   _____   _____

_____   _____   _____   _____

just	cast	past	last	mend	sack
send	pack	dust	black	bust	bend

65   Building Spelling Skills 1-2 EMC 725

Name:

Word Meaning

Fill in the missing word.

| send | back | end | both | fast |
| lasted | must | just | bath | black |

1. The ball game _____ all day.

2. We _____ be _____ by bedtime.

3. Wash _____ dogs in the _____ tub.

4. His party will _____ at 5 o'clock.

5. The _____ car was so _____ it won the race.

6. Will Uncle Fred _____ me a letter?

Write sentences with these words.

_____

_____

Building Spelling Skills

Name: _____

Word Study

Add an ending to make a word.

th   st   ck   nd

ba _____

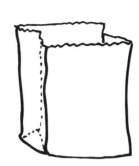

sa _____

mo _____

chi _____

bla _____

ba _____

Fill in the missing letters.

1. Put the bla ____ chi ____ in the pen with the hen.

2. He mu ____ go home soon.

3. Did you take a ba ____ ?

Building Spelling Skills 1-2 EMC 725

Name: _____

Spelling List

12

Trace	Write	Spell and Check
1. candy	_____	_____
2. went	_____	_____
3. sent	_____	_____
4. take	_____	_____
5. like	_____	_____
6. puppy	_____	_____
7. time	_____	_____
8. didn't	_____	_____
9. by	_____	_____
10. my	_____	_____
11. _____	_____	_____

fold

special word

_____
special word

Name:

Visual Memory

12

Fill in the boxes.

1.

2.

3.

4.

5.

6.

7.

8.

9.

10.

| candy | went | sent | take | like |
| time | puppy | didn't | by | my |

Name:

Contractions

12

Match:

didn't   is not

can't   did not

isn't   can not

I'm   it is

let's   I am

it's   let us

Name: _____

Word Meaning

12

Fill in the missing word.

1. It's _____ to feed the _____ .

   sent   like   puppy   time

2. _____ mom _____ me to bed.

   By   My   sent   went

3. George _____ get to _____ a turn.

   take   time   like   didn't

4. I _____ cake and _____ .

   candy   puppy   take   like

5. Jose _____ to sit _____ his dad.

   sent   by   my   went

Write sentences with these words.

_____

_____

_____

_____

 Building Spelling Skills 1-2 EMC 725

Name:

Word Study

12

Cut out the cards.
Read the words.
Paste them in the boxes.

sound of *y* in *sunny*	sound of *y* in *fly*	sound of *y* in *you*

candy	by	your
funny	my	try
happy	yell	yam
yes	fly	puppy

Name:

Spelling List

13

Trace	Write	Spell and Check
1. less	_____	_____
2. tell	_____	_____
3. well	_____	_____
4. will	_____	_____
5. still	_____	_____
6. off	_____	_____
7. letter	_____	_____
8. little	_____	_____
9. silly	_____	_____
10. happy	_____	_____
11. _____	_____	_____

fold

special word

_____

special word

     Building Spelling Skills 1-2 EMC 725

Visual Memory

Name: _____

Fill in the boxes.

1.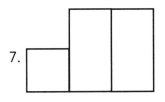

2.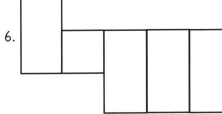

3.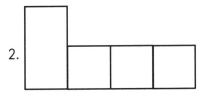

4.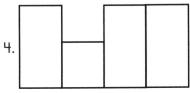

5.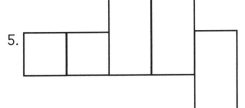

6.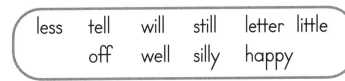

7.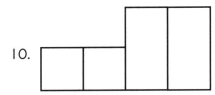

8.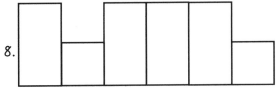

9.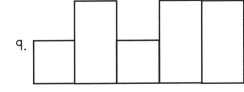

10.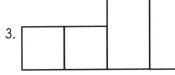

less   tell   will   still   letter   little
off   well   silly   happy

Find the Mistake

Name: _____

Put an X on the misspelled words.

1. wil   will
2. hapy   happy
3. letter   leter
4. off   oof
5. sily   silly

6. less   les
7. litle   little
8. tel   tell
9. well   wel
10. still   stell

     Building Spelling Skills 1-2 EMC 725

Building Spelling Skills

Name: _____

Word Meaning

Fill in the missing word.

1. Mom was _____ to get a _____ from Grandma.

    little   happy   letter   less

2. Can you _____ me a _____ joke?

    silly   well   tell   will

3. I _____ take a _____ bit of candy.

    well   will   letter   little

4. It is _____ hot outside in the sun.

    happy   will   still   silly

5. Turn _____ the T.V. when you go to bed.

    less   of   off   if

6. Is six _____ than ten?

    well   less   will   tell

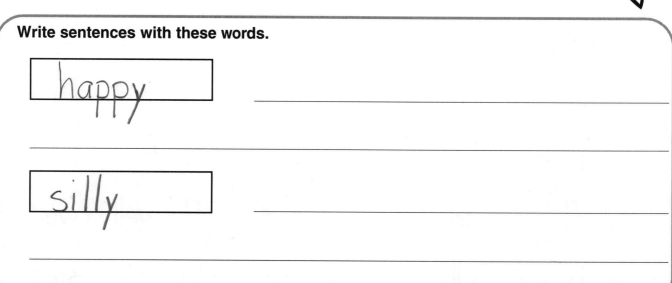

Write sentences with these words.

| happy | _____ |

| silly | _____ |

Name:

Word Study

13

Write the words that rhyme.

better   dress   four   seen

some   well   when   will

1. less _____

2. tell _____

3. still _____

4. letter _____

5. come _____

6. or _____

7. men _____

8. queen _____

How Many Syllables?

Circle the number of syllables in the word.

1. letter   1   2

2. silly   1   2

3. well   1   2

4. less   1   2

5. little   1   2

6. happy   1   2

7. still   1   2

8. rabbit   1   2

9. bunny   1   2

10. black   1   2

11. into   1   2

12. two   1   2

13. lasted   1   2

14. place   1   2

15. help   1   2

16. making   1   2

Building Spelling Skills 1-2 EMC 725

Name:

Spelling List

14

Trace	Write	Spell and Check
1. boat		
2. coat		
3. float		
4. long		
5. along		
6. belong		
7. paw		
8. fawn		
9. tall		
10. wall		
11. _____ *special word*		

fold

_____ *special word*

Building Spelling Skills

Visual Memory

14

Fill in the boxes.

1.

2.

3.

4.

5.

6.

7.

8.

9.

10.

boat	float	coat	long	along
belong	paw	fawn	tall	wall

Name:

Spell Vowel Sounds

14

Add the missing letters.

aw   all   oa

f _____ n

p _____

w _____

b _____ t

c _____ t

fl _____ t

Name:

Word Meaning

14

Fill in the missing word.

1. Can Allen _____ his _____ in the pond?
   boat   float

2. Did the _____ _____ _____ to that man?
   belong   coat   long

3. A _____ ran _____ the _____ _____.
   fawn   tall   wall   along

Write sentences with these words.

float _____

_____

belong _____

_____

Name:

Word Study

14

Cut out the cards.
Read the words.
Paste them in the boxes.

vowel sound in *song*	vowel sound in *go*

boat	so	long	fawn
tall	coat	paw	wall
note	float	fall	saw
bone	rope		

Name:

15

Trace	Write	Spell and Check
1. way		
2. away		
3. today		
4. chain		
5. wait		
6. chase		
7. play		
8. played		
9. rain		
10. paint		
11. _____		
special word		

fold

_____
special word

Building Spelling Skills

Name: _____

Fill in the boxes.

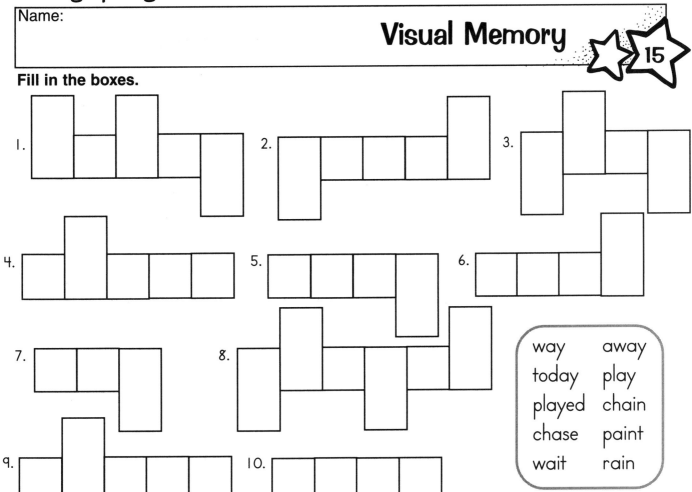

1.

2.

3.

4.

5.

6.

7.

8.

9.

10.

way	away
today	play
played	chain
chase	paint
wait	rain

Name: _____

Spell Vowel Sounds   15

What is missing—ai or ay?

ch ____ n   r ____ n   p ____ nt

1. w ____   3. pl ____

2. w ____ t   4. tod ____

Name:

Word Meaning

15

Fill in the missing word.

way	away	today	play	played
chain	chase	paint	wait	rain

1. We like to _____ kick ball.

2. Don't run _____.

3. Did Arnold's dog _____ the cat?

4. We are going to _____ the gate _____.

5. Carlos got wet in the _____.

6. Lock your bike up with that _____.

Write sentences with these words.

paint _____

_____

chain _____

_____

Building Spelling Skills

Word Study

15

Cut out the cards.

Read the words.

Paste the words that rhyme in the same box.

say	gain	vase

chain	way	chase	rain
play	case	face	away
today	pain	lane	race
main	stay	place	

Name:

Trace	**Write**	**Spell and Check**
1. too	_____	_____
2. good	_____	_____
3. book	_____	_____
4. shook	_____	_____
5. school	_____	_____
6. when	_____	_____
7. what	_____	_____
8. took	_____	_____
9. who	_____	_____
10. soon	_____	_____
11. _____	_____	_____

fold

11. _____
   special word

_____
special word

Building Spelling Skills 1-2 EMC 725

Building Spelling Skills

Fill in the boxes.

1.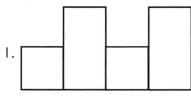

2.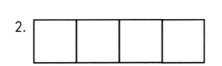

3.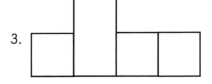

4.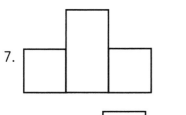

5.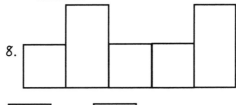

6.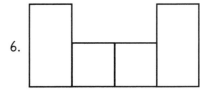

7.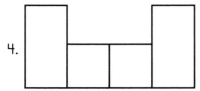

8.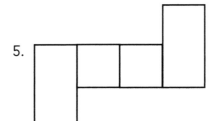

9.

10.

too	good
book	shook
school	soon
what	when
who	took

Circle the words that are spelled correctly.

1. skool (school)

2. good gud

3. shook shoock

4. hoo who

5. took twok

6. wat what

7. when wen

8. bock book

Name:

Word Meaning

16

Fill in the missing word.

too	good	book	shook	school
soon	what	when	who	took

1. It's time to go to _____.

2. Is that a _____ _____ to read?

3. He _____ the bell to make it ring.

4. _____ is the fastest runner in class?

5. Can you tell me _____ is in the box?

6. Did Zeke go swimming _____?

Write sentences with these words.

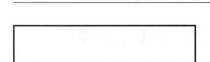

_____

_____

_____

_____

Name:

Word Study

16

Cut out the cards.
Read the words.
Paste them in the boxes.

sound of *oo* in *too*	sound of *oo* in *book*

school	good	cook
soon	shook	who
hook	to	boo
look	tool	took

     Building Spelling Skills 1-2 EMC 725

Name:

Spelling List

17

Trace	Write	Spell and Check
1. now	_____	_____
2. down	_____	_____
3. how	_____	_____
4. out	_____	_____
5. shout	_____	_____
6. about	_____	_____
7. our	_____	_____
8. house	_____	_____
9. slow	_____	_____
10. show	_____	_____
11. _____	_____	_____

special word

fold

_____

special word

Building Spelling Skills

Visual Memory

Fill in the boxes.

1.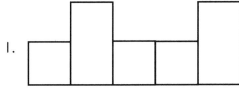

2.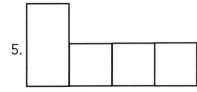

3.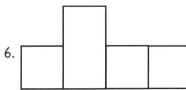

4.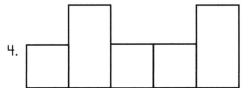

5.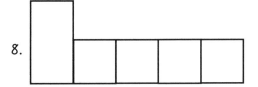

6.

7.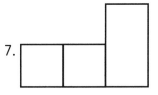

8.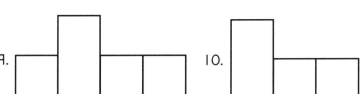

9.

10.

now	down
how	out
shout	about
our	house
slow	show

Name:

Spell Vowel Sounds

What is missing—ow or ou?

1. h _ou_ se

2. sh ___

3. d ___ n

4. sh ___ t

5. ___ t

6. n ___

7. ab ___ t

8. sl ___

Building Spelling Skills

Name:

Fill in the missing word.

> now   down   how   out   shout
> about   our   house   slow   show

1. Don't _____ in the _____.

2. Can we go home _____?

3. _____ car is too _____.

4. The little boy jumped up and _____.

5. _____ will we get to the _____?

6. This book is _____ dinosaurs.

Write sentences with these words.

| about | _____ |

_____

| show | _____ |

_____

Building Spelling Skills 1-2 EMC 725

Building Spelling Skills

Name: _____

Cut out the cards.
Read the words.
Paste them in the boxes.

sound of *ow* in *now*	sound of *o* in *no*

now	out	slow	bone
down	shout	show	how
so	row	about	grow
go	our	house	mow

Name:

Spelling List

18

Trace	Write	Spell and Check
1. her	_____	_____
2. girl	_____	_____
3. turn	_____	_____
4. hurt	_____	_____
5. first	_____	_____
6. were	_____	_____
7. card	_____	_____
8. part	_____	_____
9. start	_____	_____
10. are	_____	_____
11. _____	_____	_____

fold

special word

_____
special word

Building Spelling Skills 1-2 EMC 725

Building Spelling Skills

Name:

Visual Memory

Fill in the boxes.

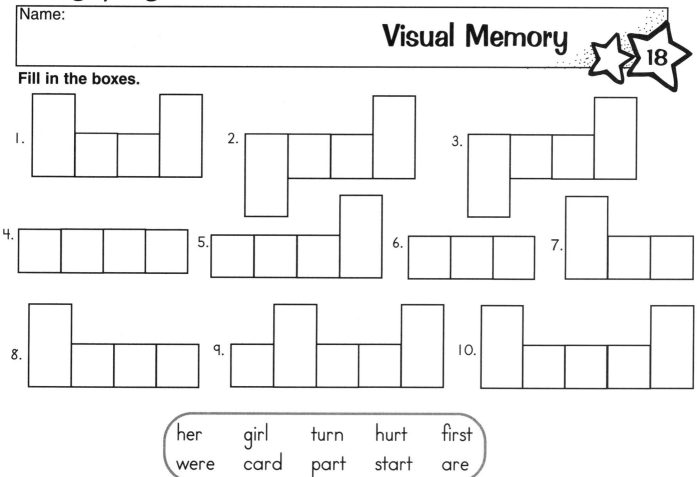

her	girl	turn	hurt	first
were	card	part	start	are

Name:

Find the Mistake

Put an X on the misspelled words.

1. That ~~gril~~ hurt her leg.

2. Did the game stard?

3. The ferst joke was funny.

4. It is Bob's tirn next.

5. Dogs and cats ar nice pets.

Name:

Word Meaning

18

Fill in the missing word.

1. She was the _____ _____ to play ball.

      hurt   her   first   girl

2. Margo _____ _____ hand when she fell.

      were   her   part   hurt

3. The girls _____ _____ of the team.

      start   part   are   were

4. _____ the game with that _____.

      Are   Start   card   star

5. The next _____ is for Kelly.

      girl   hurt   turn   were

Write sentences with these words.

hurt _____

_____

part _____

_____

Building Spelling Skills

Name:

Write the letters that spell the sound **er** in these words.

> er   ir   ur

1. h _____

2. t _____ n

3. g _____ l

4. h _____ t

5. w _____ e

6. f _____ st

7. st _____

8. c _____ l

9. t _____ key

10. n _____ se

Name:

Circle the words that are spelled correctly.

1. ar   are

2. card   kard

3. strat   start

4. part   pard

5. dark   drak

6. fer   far

7. pardy   party

8. garden   gardn

Name:

Trace	Write	Spell and Check
1. more		
2. store		
3. stand		
4. star		
5. blew		
6. flew		
7. new		
8. stone		
9. sting		
10. ring		
11. _____		

fold

special word

_____
special word

Name: _____

Visual Memory

⭐ 19

Fill in the boxes.

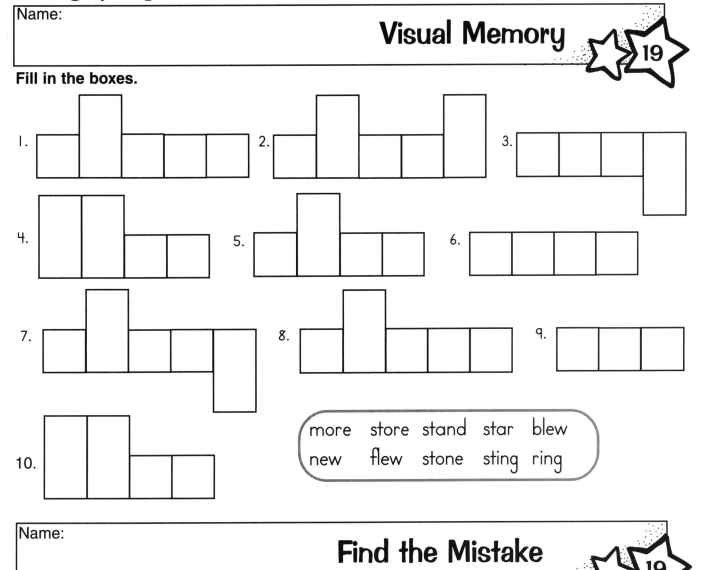

more   store   stand   star   blew
new   flew   stone   sting   ring

Name: _____

Find the Mistake

⭐ 19

Circle the misspelled words.

1. I went to the (stor) for mom.

2. He blue up a red balloon.

3. The bird flu into a tree.

4. Did a bee stinged Jamal?

5. Can I have some moor cookies?

Name: _____

Word Meaning

19

Fill in the missing word.

more	store	stand	star	blew
new	flew	stone	sting	ring

1. There is a yellow _____ on Pam's hat.

2. She got a gold _____ at the _____.

3. The blue bird _____ back to her nest.

4. Did that bee _____ you?

5. We had to _____ in line to get on the bus.

6. Herman _____ out the candles on his cake.

Write sentences with these words.

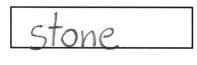

_____

_____

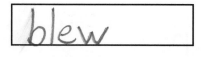

_____

_____

Building Spelling Skills

Name: _____

Write the missing letters.

st　　bl　　fl

_____ar

_____ocks

_____y

_____ackbird

_____ick

_____ag

Name: _____

Circle the letters that make the same sound as oo **in** too.

fl(ew)	moon	tool	school
you	who	do	too
to	chew	new	tooth

Name:

Spelling List

20

Trace	Write	Spell and Check
1. have		
2. give		
3. love		
4. from		
5. live		
6. friend		
7. much		
8. such		
9. old		
10. told		
11. _____		

fold

special word

_____

special word

Building Spelling Skills 1-2 EMC 725

Building Spelling Skills

Visual Memory

20

Fill in the boxes.

1.

2.

3.

4.

5.

6.

7.

8.

9.

10.

have   give   love   from   live
friend   much   such   old   told

Rhyming Words

20

Match the words that rhyme.

give   such   long   note

old   live   coat   some

much   glove   too   song

love   told   rope   bunny

from   lend   come   to

friend   some   funny   soap

Name:

Word Meaning

20

Fill in the missing word.

1. She got a letter _____ her best _____.

       told   friend   from

2. How _____ do you _____ your mother?

       love   such   much

3. Did Mark _____ in that _____ house?

       have   old   live

4. Will you _____ Donald part of your candy?

       have   live   give

5. Alex _____ me to call him after school.

       old   from   told

Write sentences with these words.

friend _____

_____

told _____

_____

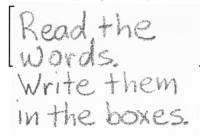

Read the
words.
Write them
in the boxes.

Word Study

20

long vowel sound	short vowel sound

stove	have	glove	gave
give	shove	five	wave
love	dive	save	above

     Building Spelling Skills 1-2 EMC 725

Name:

Spelling List

Trace	Write	Spell and Check
1. you	_____	_____
2. your	_____	_____
3. yes	_____	_____
4. yell	_____	_____
5. drop	_____	_____
6. line	_____	_____
7. side	_____	_____
8. dress	_____	_____
9. draw	_____	_____
10. saw	_____	_____
11. _____ special word	_____	_____
_____ special word		

fold

Building Spelling Skills

Name:

Fill in the boxes.

1.
2.
3.
4.
5.
6.
7.
8.
9.
10.

| you | yes | yell | drop | line |
| side | your | dress | draw | saw |

Name:

Circle the words that are spelled correctly.

1. uoo   yeew   (you)

2. dess   dress   dreds

3. side   syde   sihd

4. zaw   saw   sah

5. grop   jrop   drop

6. line   yine   lin

Building Spelling Skills

Name: _____

Fill in the missing word.

you	yes	yell	drop	line
side	your	dress	draw	saw

1. Say _____ if I can go to the party.

2. Mary wore her red _____.

3. Stand on that side of the _____.

4. Will you _____ a clown for me?

5. Use the _____ to cut that wood.

6. Don't _____ your glass of milk.

7. I will _____ if you hit me.

Write sentences with these words.

your _____

dress _____

_____

Name:

Word Study

21

Fill in the missing letters.

tr   dr   cr

_____uck

_____ess

_____ab

_____ee

_____own

_____um

_____icket

_____agon

_____umpet

tr   dr   cr

1. The baby began to ____y.

2. Put that junk in the ____ash can.

3. Don't ____ip water on the clean floor.

4. The farmer planted a new ____op of corn.

5. We rode the ____ain to New York.

Building Spelling Skills 1-2 EMC 725

Building Spelling Skills

Name:

Trace	Write	Spell and Check
1. boy	_____	_____
2. toy	_____	_____
3. oil	_____	_____
4. soil	_____	_____
5. other	_____	_____
6. mother	_____	_____
7. sister	_____	_____
8. boil	_____	_____
9. brother	_____	_____
10. father	_____	_____
11. _____ *special word*	_____	
_____ *special word*		

fold

Building Spelling Skills

Name:

Fill in the boxes.

1.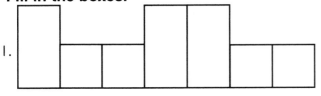

2.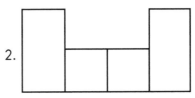

3.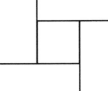

4.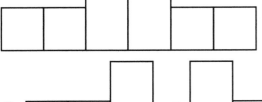

5.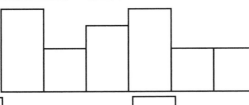

6.

7.

8.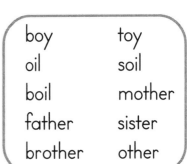

9.

10.

boy	toy
oil	soil
boil	mother
father	sister
brother	other

Name:

What is missing—oy or oi?

1. b ___

2. b ___ l

3. c ___ n

4. R ___

5. s ___ l

6. ___ l

7. t ___

8. n ___ se

1. A b ____ was digging a hole in the s ____ l.

2. The loud n ____ se woke up the baby.

3. R ____ got a t ____ truck at the store.

Building Spelling Skills 1-2 EMC 725

Name:

Word Meaning

Fill in the missing word.

boy	toy	oil	soil	boil
mother	father	sister	brother	other

1. _____ and _____ went to town.

2. Angela is my baby _____ .

3. Is that _____ your big _____?

4. The water will _____ when it gets very hot.

5. Jack likes this show, but I like the _____ one.

6. Plant seeds in the _____ in that pot.

Write sentences with these words.

Add or change letters to make new words.

b   m   s   t   br

Roy	____oy	____oy
oil	____oil	____oil
other	____other	____other
twister	____ister	____ister

Name:

Circle the number of syllables in each word.

1. boy   1 2 3   6. soil   1 2 3

2. brother 1 2 3   7. brother 1 2 3

3. boiling 1 2 3   8. family 1 2 3

4. sister 1 2 3   9. father 1 2 3

5. another 1 2 3   10. oil   1 2 3

Name:

Spelling List

23

Trace	Write	Spell and Check
1. this		
2. then		
3. thing		
4. thank		
5. bank		
6. with		
7. wish		
8. think		
9. sing		
10. these		
11. _____		

fold

special word

_____

special word

112

Name: _____

Visual Memory

Fill in the boxes.

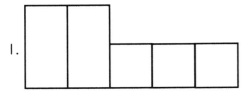

1.

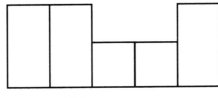

2.

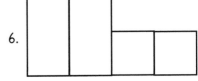

3.

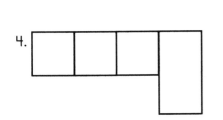

4.

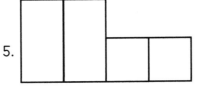

5.

6.

7.

8.

9.

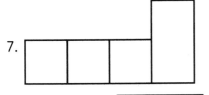

10.

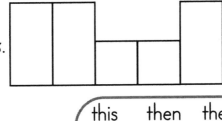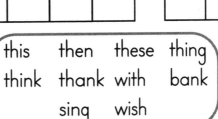

this	then	these	thing
think	thank	with	bank
	sing	wish	

Name: _____

Final Sounds

23

Add ending letters to make words.

nk   ng   sh   th

1. thi ___   thi ___

2. si ___   si ___

3. wi ___   wi ___   wi ___   wi ___

4. ba ___   ba ___   ba ___   ba ___

Name: _____

Word Meaning

23

Fill in the missing word.

> this   then   these   thing   think
> thank   with   bank   sing   wish

1. I _____ I had a new bike.

2. What is this _____ ?

3. Katy put her three dimes in her _____ .

4. Did Lara say _____ you for the present?

5. Are _____ your socks?

6. Let's _____ a funny song.

7. Did you _____ the test was hard?

8. Put the chicks in _____ the mother hen.

Write sentences with these words.

_____ _____

_____

_____ _____

_____

        Building Spelling Skills 1-2 EMC 725

Building Spelling Skills

Name: _____

Cut out the cards.
Read the words.
Paste the cards in the correct boxes.

the sound of *th* in *the*	the sound of *th* in *thin*

thank	with	this	then
thing	these	think	than
bath	those	that	thick

Name:

Spelling List

24

Trace	Write	Spell and Check
1. why		
2. try		
3. trying		
4. eat		
5. mean		
6. read		
7. sunny		
8. fly		
9. treat		
10. each		
11. _____ *special word*		

_____
special word

       Building Spelling Skills 1-2 EMC 725

fold

Building Spelling Skills

Name: _____

Fill in the boxes.

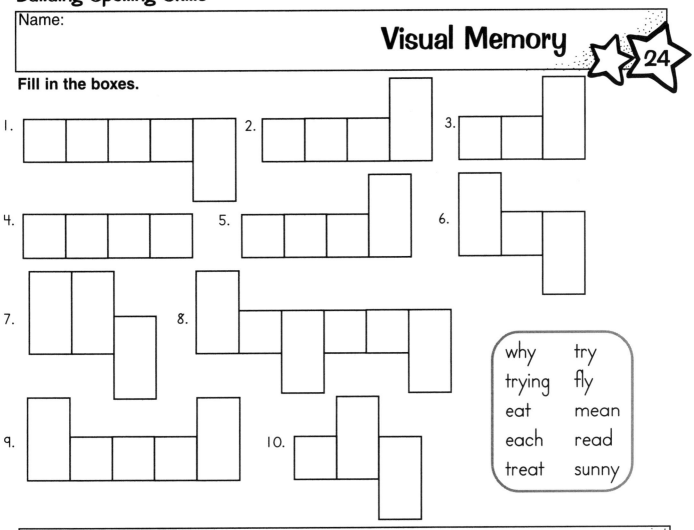

1.

2.

3.

4.

5.

6.

7.

8.

9.

10.

why	try
trying	fly
eat	mean
each	read
treat	sunny

Name: _____

Beginning Sounds

24

Change letters to make new words.

r   m   f   sh   tr   cr

fry   ___ y   funny   ___ unny   bead   ___ ead

shy   ___ y   bean   ___ ean   meat   ___ eat

Fill in the missing letters.

1. Mom gave me peanuts for a ___ eat.

2. Is it ___ unny or rainy today?

3. My baby sister started to ___ y when Mom left the room.

Name:

Word Meaning

24

Write the answers.

1. Name a **treat** you can **eat**.

   _____

2. Name three things that can **fly**.

   _____ _____ _____

3. What can you do on a **sunny** day?

   _____

4. Name two things you can **read**.

   _____ _____

5. What happens if you are **mean** to an animal?

   _____

6. Circle the word that asks a question.

   try   why   fly

Write sentences with these words.

_____

_____

Building Spelling Skills

Name:

Cut out the cards.
Read the words.
Paste them in the boxes.

long i	long e

why	I	eat	see
time	treat	keep	try
mine	mean	read	pie
fly	each	me	bike

Name:

Spelling List

25

Trace	Write	Spell and Check
1. trip	_____	_____
2. tree	_____	_____
3. say	_____	_____
4. said	_____	_____
5. hop	_____	_____
6. train	_____	_____
7. number	_____	_____
8. stop	_____	_____
9. stopped	_____	_____
10. one	_____	_____
11. _____	_____	_____

fold

special word

_____

special word

Name:

Visual Memory

25

Fill in the boxes.

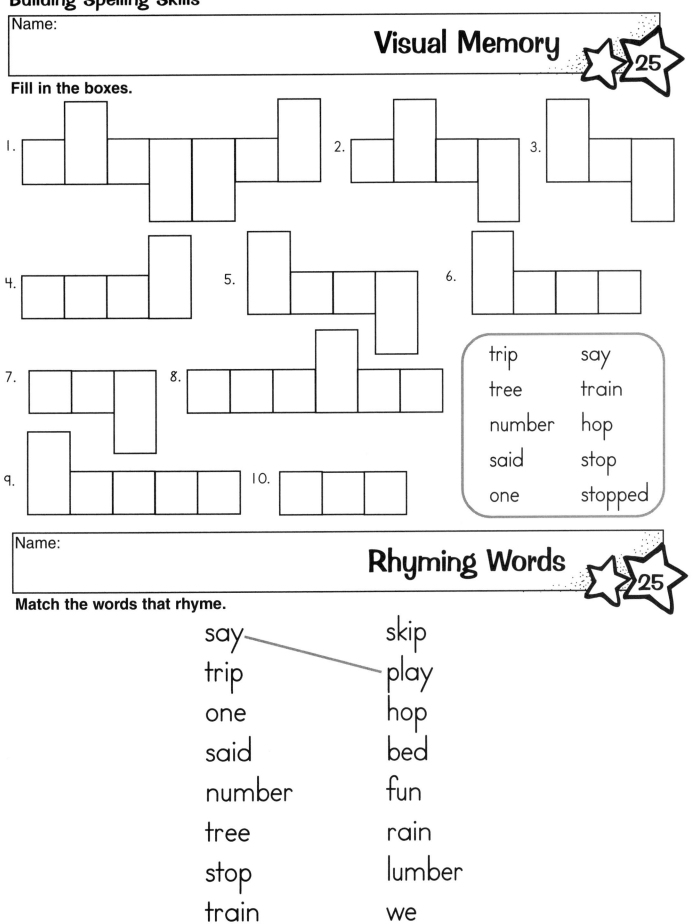

1.

2.

3.

4.

5.

6.

7.

8.

9.

10.

trip	say
tree	train
number	hop
said	stop
one	stopped

Name:

Rhyming Words

25

Match the words that rhyme.

say	skip
trip	play
one	hop
said	bed
number	fun
tree	rain
stop	lumber
train	we

Name: _____

Word Meaning

25

Fill in the missing word.

trip	say	tree	train	number
hop	said	stop	one	stopped

1. Dad _____, "Let's go out for a pizza."

2. Maria rode a _____ to her grandmother's house.

3. I saw a bunny _____ to the carrots and then

   _____ .

4. Martin was _____ _____ in the bike race.

5. They _____ by an apple _____ to rest
   in the shade.

6. What did the teacher _____ to her class?

Write sentences with these words.

	_____
	_____

Name:

Word Study

25

If a word ends in a vowel and one consonant
- **write the last letter 2 times**
- **then add *ed* to the word**

stop+p+ed = stopped

1. trip _____

2. rob _____

3. hop _____

4. pat _____

5. clap _____

6. hum _____

7. pin _____

8. plan _____

9. slip _____

10. chat _____

11. skip _____

12. drum _____

Fill in the missing words.

1. Ann _____ down the street.

2. He _____ on the ice.

3. Dad _____ a trip.

4. The bad man _____ a bank.

         Building Spelling Skills 1-2 EMC 725

Name:

Trace	Write	Spell and Check
1. stick	_____	_____
2. trick	_____	_____
3. back	_____	_____
4. zoo	_____	_____
5. root	_____	_____
6. quick	_____	_____
7. look	_____	_____
8. looked	_____	_____
9. pack	_____	_____
10. cook	_____	_____
11. _____	_____	_____

fold

special word

_____

special word

Name:

Visual Memory

26

Fill in the boxes.

1.

2.

3.

4.

5.

6.

7.

8.

9.

10.

stick	trick	quick
back	zoo	root
look	looked	pack
	cook	

Name:

Rhyming Words

26

Match the words that rhyme.

stick	back	trick
look	who	tack
pack	quick	cook
zoo	tool	shoot
root	book	too
school	boot	pool

Name:

Word Meaning

26

Fill in the missing word.

1. Roy _____ for his homework.

        look   looked   quick

2. Mr. Green did a _____ with a big _____ .

        stick   trick   quick

3. The chef will _____ dinner.

        look   cook   root

4. That weed had one long _____.

        look   cook   root

5. Put the _____ in the _____ seat of the car.

        back   pack   look

6. Will you help me _____ for my book?

        look   cook   book

Write sentences with these words.

Building Spelling Skills

Name: _____

What is missing—k or ck?

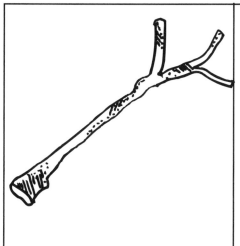

sti _____

clo _____

coo _____

du _____

boo _____

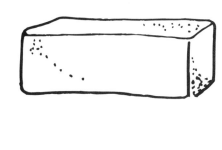

bri _____

1. loo ___

2. qui ___

3. ba ___

4. ro ___

5. hoo ___

6. pa ___

7. so ___

8. ta ___

9. haw ___

Name:

Spelling List

27

Trace	Write	Spell and Check
1. birthday	_____	_____
2. people	_____	_____
3. present	_____	_____
4. candle	_____	_____
5. cake	_____	_____
6. children	_____	_____
7. gifts	_____	_____
8. party	_____	_____
9. game	_____	_____
10. bring	_____	_____
11. _____	_____	_____

fold

special word

_____

special word

Building Spelling Skills

Name: _____

Visual Memory

Fill in the boxes.

1.
2.
3.
4.
5.
6.
7.
8.
9.
10.

people	present
candle	cake
children	birthday
party	game
bring	gifts

Name: _____

Find Words Inside Words

Use small words you know to help you spell new words.

g _____ t

_____ dle

_____ ren

Circle small words in these spelling words.

present   party   bring   birthday

Building Spelling Skills

Name: _____

27

Answer the questions.

1. Are children people?	Yes No
2. Do present and gift mean the same thing?	Yes No
3. Can you eat the candles on a birthday cake?	Yes No
4. Will your mother let you play a card game in the house?	Yes No
5. Do people bring presents to a birthday party?	Yes No
6. Is your birthday the day your mother was born?	Yes No

Write sentences with these words.

[_____] _____

_____

[_____] _____

_____

Name: _____

Word Study

 27

What letters are missing?

pr   br   ch

____ esent

____ air

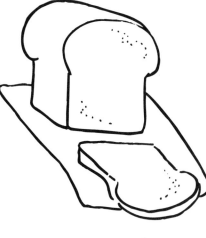

____ ead

____ idge

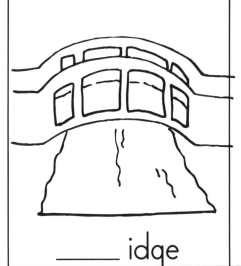

____ incess

____ ips

1. _____ etty

2. _____ ing

3. _____ ick

4. _____ ain

5. _____ ize

6. _____ own

   Building Spelling Skills 1-2 EMC 725

Name:

Trace	Write	Spell and Check
1. put		
2. push		
3. pull		
4. could		
5. would		
6. found		
7. round		
8. around		
9. something		
10. brown		
11. _____ special word		

_____
special word

fold

Name: _____

Visual Memory

Fill in the boxes.

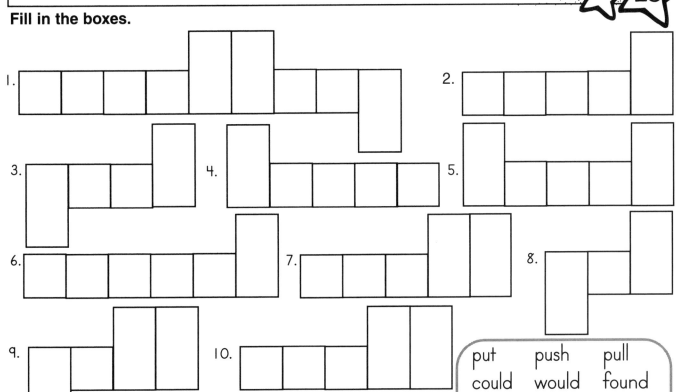

put	push	pull
could	would	found
round	brown	around
	something	

Name: _____

Spell Vowel Sounds

What is missing—ou or ow?

1. f _ou_ nd

2. r _____ nd

3. br _____ n

4. cl _____ n

5. ar _____ nd

6. c _____

7. s _____ nd

8. c _____ nt

9. d _____ n

10. t _____ n

Name: _____

Word Meaning

28

Fill in the missing word.

put	push	pull	could	would
found	round	around	something	brown

1. Otis _____ his lost dog.

2. Betty hit the ball and ran _____ the bases.

3. She saw _____ funny on T. V.

4. Will you help me _____ my sled up the hill?

5. That rock is _____ with _____ spots.

6. Burt said he _____ help paint the fence.

Write sentences with these words.

[ ] _____

_____

[ ] _____

_____

Building Spelling Skills

Word Study

28

Cut out the cards.
Read the words.
Paste them in the boxes.

the sound of *ow* in *cow*	the sound of *oo* in *wood*

round	put	push	brown
could	hood	sound	pull
town	now	would	found

Name:

Trace	Write	Spell and Check
1. they	_____	_____
2. their	_____	_____
3. many	_____	_____
4. any	_____	_____
5. anything	_____	_____
6. than	_____	_____
7. because	_____	_____
8. know	_____	_____
9. water	_____	_____
10. very	_____	_____
11. _____	_____	_____

fold

special word

_____
special word

Building Spelling Skills

Name: _____

Visual Memory

Fill in the boxes.

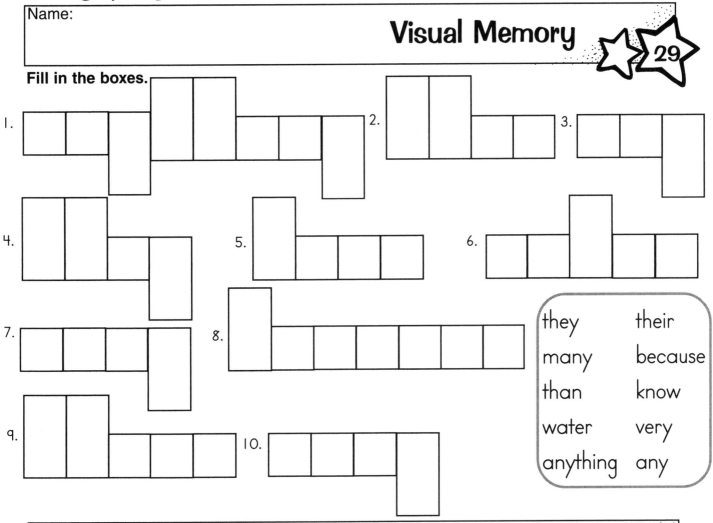

they   their

many   because

than   know

water   very

anything   any

Name: _____

Find the Mistake

Put an X on the words that are misspelled.

1. en~~y~~thing   anything

2. because   becuz

3. kno   know

4. thay   they

5. water   wadder

6. miny   many

7. verry   very

8. any   iny

Name:

Word Meaning

29

Fill in the missing word.

1. Grandpa said, "You may have _____ you want."

   anything   many   any

2. Do you _____ how _____ fish are in the tank?

   know   no   many

3. Fill the glass with cold _____ .

   winter   water   what

4. It is _____ hot _____ the sun is shining.

   very   any   because

5. Put _____ coats over _____ .

   they   there   their

6. When will _____ get here?

   they   than   them

Write sentences with these words.

☐ _____

☐ _____

Name: _____

Word Study

29

Circle the sound made by the underlined letters.

1. th<u>ey</u>   a e i o   9. pr<u>ey</u>   a e i o
2. th<u>ei</u>r   a e i o   10. s<u>o</u>   a e i o
3. an<u>y</u>   a e i o   11. man<u>y</u>   a e i o
4. kn<u>ow</u>   a e i o   12. m<u>y</u>   a e i o
5. n<u>i</u>ne   a e i o   13. pl<u>ay</u>   a e i o
6. ver<u>y</u>   a e i o   14. p<u>ie</u>   a e i o
7. s<u>ee</u>   a e i o   15. b<u>o</u>ne   a e i o
8. c<u>oa</u>t   a e i o   16. m<u>ea</u>t   a e i o

Name: _____

Word Study

29

Fill in the missing word.

1. Do you _____ how to swim?   no   know

_____, you can't go swimming now.   No   Know

2. I have _____ goldfish in my tank.   to   two

Can we go _____ the zoo next Saturday?   to   two

3. Did you see _____ new puppy?   there   their

Put your wet boots over_____.   there   their

                   Building Spelling Skills 1-2 EMC 725

Name:

Spelling List

30

Trace	Write	Spell and Check
1. which	_____	_____
2. where	_____	_____
3. there	_____	_____
4. before	_____	_____
5. after	_____	_____
6. over	_____	_____
7. again	_____	_____
8. inside	_____	_____
9. outside	_____	_____
10. under	_____	_____
11. _____ special word	_____	_____

_____
special word

fold

Building Spelling Skills

Name: _____

Visual Memory

Fill in the boxes.

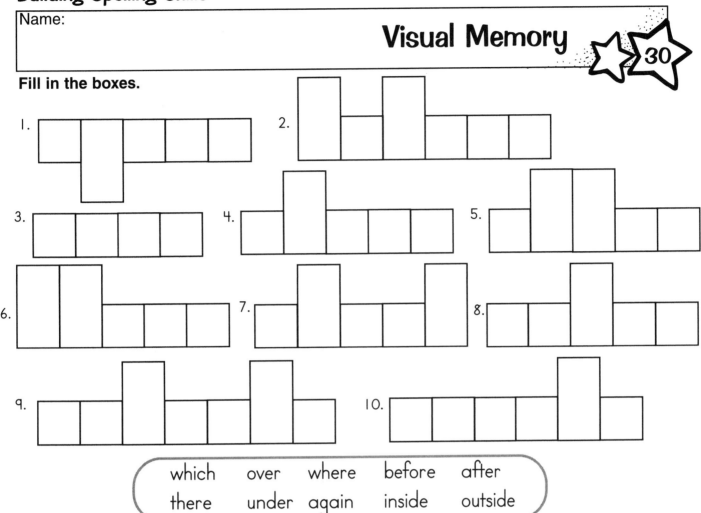

1.
2.
3.
4.
5.
6.
7.
8.
9.
10.

which   over   where   before   after
there   under   again   inside   outside

Name: _____

Opposites

Write the word that means the opposite.

1. over _____

2. yes _____

3. inside _____

4. push _____

5. here _____

6. quick _____

7. before _____

8. new _____

Name:

Word Meaning

Look at the picture. Answer the question.

Is the cat hiding under the bed?

Yes
No

Is the clown before the elephant?

Yes
No

Is the cover over the birdcage?

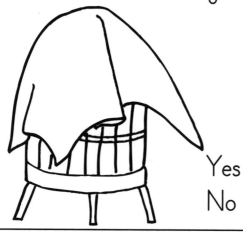

Yes
No

Has the dog gone inside its doghouse?

dog

Yes
No

Will you wear your raincoat when you go outside?

Yes
No

Will you need a bath after digging in the garden?

Yes
No

Name: _____

Word Study

30

Put two words together to make a new word.

in + side   <u>inside</u>

1. any + thing _____   4. in + to _____

2. out + side _____   5. be + side _____

3. some + thing _____   6. no + thing _____

Circle the two words in these compound words.
Draw a picture of each word.

butterfly	cowboy	goldfish
bathtub	cupcake	rainbow

     Building Spelling Skills 1-2 EMC 725

Spelling Record Sheet

Spelling List Number	Student Names														
1															
2															
3															
4															
5															
6															
7															
8															
9															
10															
11															
12															
13															
14															
15															
16															
17															
18															
19															
20															
21															
22															
23															
24															
25															
26															
27															
28															
29															
30															

Individual Spelling Record

Date	Spelling List	Number Correct	Words Missed	Comments

 Building Spelling Skills 1-2 EMC 725

Spelling

1. _____

2. _____

3. _____

4. _____

5. _____

6. _____

7. _____

8. _____

9. _____

10. _____

11. _____

12. _____

Review Words

1. _____   2. _____   3. _____

 ## Sentence Dictation

1. _____

_____

2. _____

Name:

Spelling List

Trace	Write	Spell and Check
1.	_____	_____
2.	_____	_____
3.	_____	_____
4.	_____	_____
5.	_____	_____
6.	_____	_____
7.	_____	_____
8.	_____	_____
9.	_____	_____
10.	_____	_____
11. _____ *special word*	_____	_____
12. _____ *special word*	_____	_____

fold

Building Spelling Skills

Word Box

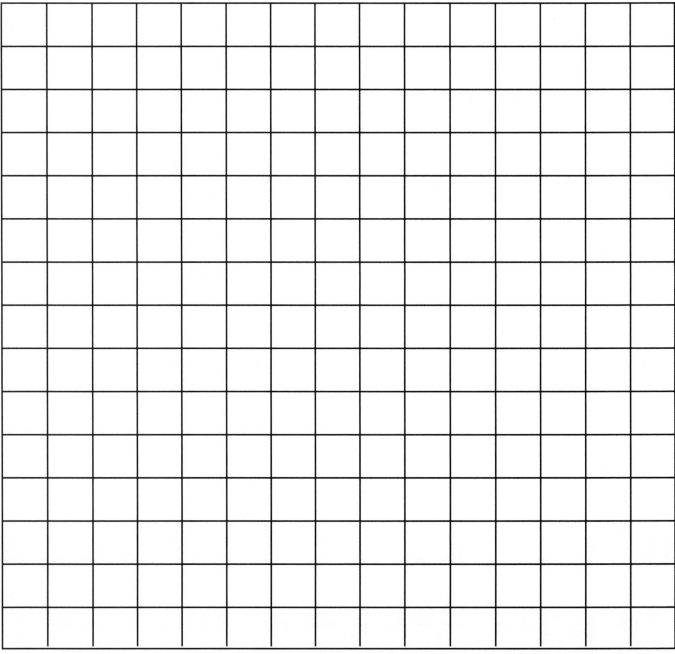

Word Sort

Cut out the cards.
Read the words.
Paste them in the boxes.

Dear Parents,

Attached is your child's spelling list for this week. Encourage him/her to practice the words in one or more of these ways.

1. Read and spell each word. Cover it up and write it. Uncover the word and check to see if it is correct.

2. Find the words on the spelling list in printed materials such as books and magazines.

3. You read a word aloud and ask your child to spell it (either aloud or written on paper).

Thank you for your support of our spelling program.

Sincerely,

Dear Parents,

Attached is your child's spelling list for this week. Encourage him/her to practice the words in one or more of these ways.

1. Read and spell each word. Cover it up and write it. Uncover the word and check to see if it is correct.

2. Find the words on the spelling list in printed materials such as books and magazines.

3. You read a word aloud and ask your child to spell it (either aloud or written on paper).

Thank you for your support of our spelling program.

Sincerely,

Answer Key

Page 25
1. but, hat, did, or hot
2. but, hat, did, or hot
3. but, hat, did, or hot
4. get
5. in or on
6. at
7. in or on
8. not or red
9. but, hat, did, or hot
10. red or not

1. The pan is hat.
2. A dog is un the bed.
3. Can I git a cat?
4. His hat is read.

Page 26
1. red
2. on
3. get
4. Did
5. hot
6. had

Page 27

a	e	i	o	u
at	get	in	on	but
had	red	did	not	cup
pan	men	sit	hot	up

Page 29
1. big
2. fox, box, or has
3. nap
4. egg
5. jam
6. fox, box, or has
7. as
8. fox, box, or has
9. pet
10. mix

fox	jam	box	egg
as	has	mix	
nap	pet	big	

Page 30
1. fox   box
2. big   egg
3. jam
4. has   nap
5. mix
6. pet

Page 31
1. jam   nap   has
2. pet   egg   red
3. box   fox   got
4. it   mix   rip

1.	fox	box
2.	has	as
3.	get	pet
4.	pig	big
5.	fix	mix

Page 33
1. small
2. land or hand
3. and
4. all
5. his
6. can
7. is or an
8. land or hand
9. call
10. is or an

an	small	can
is	and	hand
call	his	all
land		

Page 34
1. small
2. hand
3. land
4. call
5. all
6. his

Page 35

a in an	a in all
can	small
cat	fawn
and	call
has	want
land	saw
hand	ball

Page 37
1. man or men
2. him or for
3. it
4. man or men
5. him or for
6. we or or
7. up
8. four
9. we or or
10. I

1. Tim has (for) dogs.
2. That (min) had a hat.
3. Can (wee) go with them?
4. Is the cake (four) me?
5. Did Nina see (hem)?

Page 38
1. four
2. for
3. man
4. men
5. I
6. up

Page 39

man	can	fan
hen	men	pen
coat	boat	goat

Page 41
1. save, name, came, or mine
2. cute or ride
3. ask
4. ride or cute
5. save, name, came, or mine
6. add
7. save, name, came, or mine
8. bone
9. kite
10. save, name, came, or mine

1. came
2. ask
3. kite
4. ride
5. cute
6. bone
7. mine
8. add
9. save
10. name

Page 42
1. cute
2. Save   bone
3. kite   mine
4. ask   ride
5. name

Page 43
long	short
came	add
ride	up
save	him
cute	men
bone	ask
name	can
mine	got
kite	hand

Page 45
1. sheep
2. shop
3. be or he
4. she
5. bee
6. got
7. he or be
8. queen
9. been
10. see

queen   sheep   bee

1. see
2. he
3. been
4. be
5. she
6. peep

Page 46
1. queen   sheep
2. She
3. shop

1. been
2. bee
3. he   see

Page 47
e in me	e in pet
be	get
see	hen
queen	mess
she	bell
sheep	red
bee	then

Page 49
1. doing
2. most
3. no or so
4. gave
5. kind or find
6. do
7. go
8. going
9. kind or find
10. so or no

no-so or go
mind-find or kind
cave-gave
post-most

go-going   find-finding
do-doing   sleep-sleeping

Page 50
1. doing
2. kind
3. going
4. gave
5. most
6. find
7. to

Page 51
o in no	o in too
most	to
so	blue
go	do

i in my	a in cave
kind	gave
find	cake
mine	save

Page 53
1. them
2. made
3. the
4. a
5. day
6. that
7. if or of
8. was
9. may
10. if or of

1. that
2. may
3. the
4. made
5. was
6. day
7. them
8. of

Page 54
1. day
2. a
3. may
4. made
5. the
6. that or the
7. if
8. was

Page 55

a in came		a in hat	
may	flake	sand	
stay	game	pan	
play	cape	sat	
day	cake	plant	

Page 57

1. funny
2. some or come
3. fun
4. some or come
5. run, use, or ran
6. run, use, or ran
7. us
8. running
9. home
10. run, use, or ran

1. running	5. cutting
2. hitting	6. tapping
3. humming	7. rubbing
4. tagging	8. sitting

Page 58

1. us
2. ran
3. running
4. come
5. funny
6. Some
7. fun
8. home

Page 59

u in up	o in no
some	home
fun	stone
come	bone
jump	don't
run	joke
us	boat

Page 61

1. making
2. help
3. want
4. nice
5. into or make
6. make or into
7. to
8. place
9. here
10. two

1. hep help
2. make mak
3. intwo into
4. nize nice
5. place plaic
6. makking making
7. twe two
8. here heer
9. wunt want
10. to tou

Page 62

1. help make
2. nice
3. want two
4. to
5. into
6. Here place

Page 63

1. baking
2. wanting
3. singing
4. riding
5. taking
6. starting
7. washing
8. coming
9. chasing
10. smiling

The clown is smiling.
Dad is baking.
Anna is singing.

Page 65

1. black
2. last
3. just
4. fast or back
5. must or send
6. back or fast
7. end
8. send or must
9. both or bath
10. both or bath

back	end
black	send
sack	mend
pack	bend

fast	must
last	just
cast	dust
past	bust

Page 66

1. lasted
2. must back
3. both bath
4. end
5. black fast
6. send

Page 67

ba<u>th</u> sa<u>ck</u> mo<u>th</u>
chi<u>ck</u> bla<u>ck</u> ba<u>nd</u>

1. bla<u>ck</u> chi<u>ck</u>
2. mu<u>st</u>
3. ba<u>th</u>

Page 69
1. didn't
2. take or like
3. by
4. sent or went
5. time
6. take or like
7. my
8. candy
9. puppy
10. sent or went

didn't — is not
can't — did not
isn't — can not
I'm — it is
let's — I am
it's — let us

Page 70
1. time   puppy
2. My   sent
3. didn't   take
4. like   candy
5. went   by

Page 71
y in sunny	y in fly	y in you
candy	by	yell
puppy	fly	yes
happy	my	your
funny	try	yam

Page 73
1. letter
2. less
3. will or well
4. tell
5. silly
6. happy
7. off
8. little
9. still
10. will or well

1. wil will
2. hapy happy
3. letter leter
4. off oof
5. sily silly
6. less les
7. litle little
8. tel tell
9. well wel
10. still stell

Page 74
1. happy   letter
2. tell   silly
3. will   little
4. still
5. off
6. less

Page 75
1. dress   5. some
2. well   6. four
3. will   7. when
4. better   8. seen

Page 76
1. 2   9. 2
2. 2   10. 1
3. 1   11. 2
4. 1   12. 1
5. 2   13. 2
6. 2   14. 1
7. 1   15. 1
8. 2   16. 2

Page 77
1. belong
2. along
3. long
4. coat
5. fawn
6. boat
7. paw
8. float
9. tall
10. wall

fawn	paw	wall
boat	coat	float

Page 78
1. float   boat
2. long   coat   belong
3. fawn   along   tall   wall

Page 79
song	go
long	boat
fawn	so
tall	coat
paw	note
wall	float
fall	bone
saw	rope

Page 81
1. today
2. paint
3. play
4. chase
5. away
6. wait
7. way
8. played
9. chain
10. rain

chain	rain	paint

1. way   3. play
2. wait   4. today

Page 82
1. play
2. away
3. chase
4. paint   today
5. rain
6. chain

Page 83
say	pain	vase
way	chain	chase
play	rain	case
away	pain	face
today	lane	race
stay	main	place

Page 85

1. what
2. soon
3. when
4. book or took
5. good
6. book or took
7. who
8. shook
9. school
10. too

1. school	5. took
2. good	6. what
3. shook	7. when
4. who	8. book

Page 86

1. school
2. good   book
3. shook
4. Who
5. what
6. too

Page 87

oo - too	oo - book
school	good
soon	cook
who	shook
to	hook
boo	look
tool	took

Page 89

1. about or shout
2. our or now
3. our or now
4. about or shout
5. down
6. slow
7. out
8. house
9. show
10. how

1. h<u>ou</u>se   5. <u>out</u>
2. sh<u>ow</u>   6. n<u>ow</u>
3. d<u>ow</u>n   7. ab<u>out</u>
4. sh<u>out</u>   8. sl<u>ow</u>

Page 90

1. shout   house
2. now
3. Our   slow
4. down
5. How   show
6. about

Page 91

ow - now	o - no
now	slow
out	bone
down	show
shout	so
how	row
about	grow
our	go
house	mow

Page 93

1. hurt
2. part or girl
3. girl or part
4. were
5. card
6. are
7. her
8. turn
9. start
10. first

1. That gril hurt her leg.
2. Did the game stard?
3. The ferst joke was funny.
4. It is Bob's tirn next.
5. Dogs and cats ar nice pets.

Page 94

1. first   girl
2. hurt   her
3. are   part
4. Start   card
5. turn

Page 95

1. h<u>er</u>	6. f<u>ir</u>st
2. t<u>ur</u>n	7. st<u>ir</u>
3. g<u>ir</u>l	8. c<u>ur</u>l
4. h<u>ur</u>t	9. t<u>ur</u>key
5. w<u>er</u>e	10. n<u>ur</u>se

1. are	5. dark
2. card	6. far
3. start	7. party
4. part	8. garden

Page 97

1. stone or store
2. stand
3. ring
4. flew or blew
5. star
6. more
7. sting
8. stone or store
9. new
10. flew or blew

1. I went to the stor for Mom.
2. He blue up a red balloon.
3. The bird flu into a tree.
4. Did a bee stinged Jamal?
5. Can I have some moor cookies?

Page 98

1. star
2. ring   store
3. flew
4. sting
5. stand
6. blew

Page 99

<u>star</u> <u>blocks</u> <u>fly</u>
<u>blackbird</u> <u>stick</u> <u>flag</u>

flew   moon   tool   school
you   who   do   too
to   chew   new   tooth

Page 101
1. friend
2. from, love, have, or live
3. from, love, have, or live
4. give
5. told
6. such or much
7. old
8. from, love, have, or live
9. from, love, have, or live
10. such or much

give — such
old — live
much — glove
love — told
from — lend
friend — some

long — note
coat — some
too — song
rope — bunny
come — to
funny — soap

Page 102
1. from   friend
2. much   love
3. live   old
4. give
5. told

Page 103

long vowel	short vowel
stove	have
five	glove
wave	above
dive	give
gave	love
save	shove

Page 105
1. dress
2. line or draw
3. you or yes
4. line or draw
5. your

6. yell
7. saw
8. side
9. drop
10. you or yes

1. you
2. dress
3. side
4. saw
5. drop
6. line

Page 106
1. yes
2. dress
3. line
4. draw
5. saw
6. drop
7. yell

Page 107

truck   dress   crab
tree   crown   drum
cricket dragon trumpet

1. cry
2. trash
3. drip
4. crop
5. train

Page 109
1. brother
2. boil
3. boy or toy
4. mother
5. other
6. soil
7. oil
8. father
9. sister
10. boy or toy

1. boy   4. Roy   7. toy
2. boil   5. soil   8. noise
3. coin   6. oil

boy   soil
noise
Roy   toy

Page 110
1. Mother   father
2. sister
3. boy   brother
4. boil
5. other
6. soil

Page 111
Roy   boy   toy
oil   boil   soil
other   mother   brother
twister   sister   mister
1. 1
2. 2
3. 2
4. 2
5. 3
6. 1
7. 2
8. 3
9. 2
10. 1

Page 113
1. these
2. thank or think
3. bank
4. sing
5. this or then
6. this or then
7. wish
8. thank or think
9. thing
10. with

1. think   thing
2. sink   sing
3. wink   wing   wish   with
4. bank   bang   bash   bath

Page 114
1. wish
2. thing
3. bank
4. thank
5. these
6. sing
7. think
8. with

Page 115

th - the	th - thin
this	thank
then	with
these	thing
than	think
those	bath
that	thick

Page 117
1. sunny
2. read or each
3. eat
4. mean
5. each or read
6. try
7. fly
8. trying
9. treat
10. why

fry	try	funny	sunny
bead	read	shy	cry
bean	mean	meat	treat

1. treat
2. sunny
3. cry

Page 118
Questions 1-5—answers will vary
6. why

Page 119

long i	long e
why	eat
I	see
time	treat
try	keep
mine	mean
pie	read
fly	each
bike	me

Page 121
1. stopped
2. stop
3. hop
4. said
5. trip
6. tree
7. say
8. number
9. train
10. one

say — skip
trip — play
one — hop
said — bed
number — fun
tree — rain
stop — lumber
train — we

Page 122
1. said
2. train
3. hop   stop
4. number   one
5. stopped   tree
6. say

Page 123
1. tripped
2. robbed
3. hopped
4. patted
5. clapped
6. hummed
7. pinned
8. planned
9. slipped
10. chatted
11. skipped
12. drummed

1. skipped or hopped
2. slipped
3. planned
4. robbed

Page 125
1. looked
2. stick
3. root or cook
4. root or cook
5. pack
6. look or back
7. zoo
8. trick
9. quick
10. look or back

stick   back   trick
look   who   tack
pack   quick   cook
zoo   tool   shoot
root   book   too
school   boot   pool

Page 126
1. looked
2. trick   stick
3. cook
4. root
5. pack   back
6. look

Page 127

stick   clock   cook
duck   book   brick

1. look
2. quick
3. back
4. rock
5. hook
6. pack
7. sock
8. tack
9. hawk

Page 129
1. bring
2. gifts
3. party
4. children
5. birthday
6. candle
7. cake
8. game
9. people
10. present

gift   candle   children
present   bring
party   birthday
(circled: present, party, bring, birthday)

Page 130
1. yes
2. yes
3. no
4. answers will vary
5. yes
6. no

Page 131
present   chair   bread
bridge   princess   chips

1. pretty   4. chain
2. bring   5. prize
3. chick or   6. brown
   brick

Page 133
1. something
2. round
3. push
4. brown
5. found
6. around
7. would or could
8. put
9. pull
10. would or could

1. found   6. cow
2. round   7. sound
3. brown   8. count
4. clown   9. down
5. around   10. town

Page 134
1. found
2. around
3. something
4. pull
5. round brown
6. would

Page 135
ow - cow   oo - wood
round   put
brown   push
sound   could
town   hood
now   pull
found   would

Page 137
1. anything
2. than
3. any
4. they
5. know
6. water
7. very or many
8. because
9. their
10. many or very

1. enything   anything
2. because   becuz
3. kno   know
4. thay   they
5. water   wadder
6. miny   many
7. verry   very
8. any   iny
(words with X marks crossing out misspellings)

Page 138
1. anything
2. know many
3. water
4. very because
5. their there
6. they

Page 139
1. a   9. a
2. a   10. o
3. e   11. e
4. o   12. i
5. i   13. a
6. e   14. i
7. e   15. o
8. o   16. e

1. know   No
2. two   to
3. their   there

Page 141
1. again
2. before
3. over
4. where
5. after
6. there
7. which
8. under
9. outside
10. inside

1. under   5. there
2. no   6. slow
3. outside   7. after
4. pull   8. old

Page 142
yes   yes
yes   no
no   yes

Page 143
1. anything   4. into
2. outside   5. beside
3. something   6. nothing

(circled: butterfly, cowboy, goldfish, bathtub, cupcake, rainbow)

Building Spelling Skills 1-2 EMC 725

Master Word List

a	brother	float	if
about	brown	fly	in
add	but	for	inside
after	by	found	into
again	cake	four	is
all	call	fox	it
along	came	friend	jam
an	can	from	just
and	candle	fun	kind
any	candy	funny	kite
anything	card	game	know
are	chain	gave	land
around	chase	get	last
as	children	gifts	less
ask	coat	girl	letter
at	come	give	like
away	cook	go	liked
back	could	going	line
bank	cute	good	little
bath	day	got	live
be	did	had	long
because	didn't	hand	look
bee	do	happy	looked
been	doing	has	love
before	down	have	made
belong	draw	he	make
big	dress	help	making
birthday	drop	her	man
black	each	here	many
blew	eat	him	may
boat	egg	his	mean
boil	end	home	men
bone	fast	hop	mine
book	father	house	mix
both	fawn	hot	more
box	find	how	most
boy	first	hurt	mother
bring	flew	I	much

must
my
name
nap
new
nice
no
not
now
number
of
off
oil
old
on
one
or
other
our
out
outside
over
pack
paint
part
party
paw
people
pet
place
play
played
present
pull
puppy
push
put
queen
quick

rain
ran
read
red
ride
ring
root
round
run
running
sack
said
save
saw
say
school
see
send
sent
she
sheep
shook
shop
shout
show
side
silly
sing
sister
slow
small
so
soil
some
something
soon
stand
star
start

stick
still
sting
stone
stop
stopped
store
such
sunny
take
tall
tell
than
thank
that
the
their
them
then
there
these
they
thing
think
this
time
to
today
told
too
took
toy
train
treat
tree
trick
trip
try
trying

turn
two
under
up
us
use
very
wait
wall
want
was
water
way
we
well
went
were
what
when
where
which
who
why
will
wish
with
would
yell
yes
you
your
zoo